INDEPENDENT AND UNOFFICIAL

THE ESSENTIAL
MINECRAFT
DUNGEONS
GUIDE

MORTIMER

Published in 2020 by Mortimer Children's Books
An imprint of Welbeck Children's Limited
20 Mortimer Street, London W1T 3JW
Text and design © Welbeck Children's Limited, part of
Welbeck Publishing Group.

All information correct as of July 2020.

ISBN: 978 1 83935 067 2

Printed in Dongguan, China

1 3 5 7 9 10 8 6 4 2

Writer: Tom Phillips
Designer: Dani Lurie
Design Manager: Sam James
Editorial Manager: Joff Brown
Production: Gary Hayes

THE ESSENTIAL
MINECRAFT
DUNGEONS
GUIDE

MORTIMER

CONTENTS

3. SECRET LEVELS

4. MOBPEDIA

5. THE BEST GEAR

6. BECOME A DUNGEON MASTER!

GETTING STARTED

Welcome to your essential guide for Minecraft Dungeons!
Here's how to get a head start, from the very first moment you
begin playing.

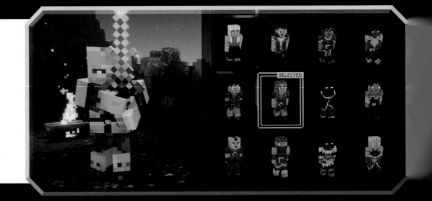

The first thing to do is
choose your avatar—the
character you will play as.
It won't make a difference
to your skills and powers
in the game, so feel free to
choose whichever you like!

You'll begin in Squid Coast, a village that is being invaded by Illagers. Will this give you
your first clue to the lair of the infamous Arch-Illager?

PILLAGE THE VILLAGE!

Never heard of the Arch-Illager before? He's a new character created specially for Minecraft Dungeons. Once a lowly Illager, looting villages across the map, he found his way into a secret dungeon where a magical artifact gave him terrifying powers! It's up to you to stop him ... if you can!

Watch for the yellow on-screen arrow, which will always show you where to go next. Following it will help you keep your bearings and stop you from getting lost.

Watch out for these little guys —they're key golems. Catching one will get you into the next section of the dungeon. But if you're hit, you'll drop it, and it'll run off! So hold it tight...

WHAT'S ON SCREEN

To get anywhere in Minecraft Dungeons, you'll need to know what's going on on-screen ... here's how it works!

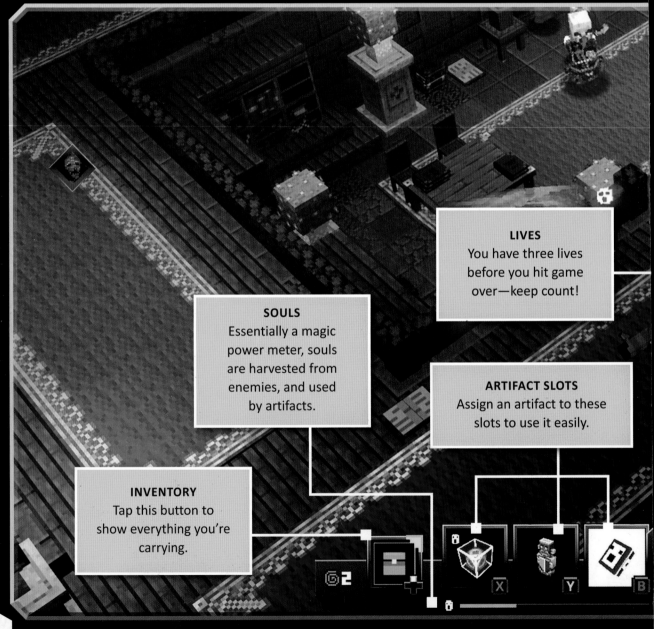

LIVES
You have three lives before you hit game over—keep count!

SOULS
Essentially a magic power meter, souls are harvested from enemies, and used by artifacts.

ARTIFACT SLOTS
Assign an artifact to these slots to use it easily.

INVENTORY
Tap this button to show everything you're carrying.

ENEMIES
Any enemies that you can hit will be outlined in red.

WAYPOINT
Follow this marker to lead you to your next objective.

YOU
That's you—or at least your avatar! You'll always be in the center of the screen.

HEALTH
Keep an eye on your health—if it starts to drop, you're in trouble.

ARROWS
If you're playing with a gamepad, your ranged weapon is mapped to the right trigger.

HEALTH POTION
Health potions are unlimited, but take time to recharge.

EMERALDS
Collect emeralds and spend them to get essential upgrades.

LV **36**

LB   RB   RT   54   6890

FIGHTING CHANCE

Heavy-hitting dungeon explorers use these tips to give them the edge in combat!

Zombies come in large hordes—avoid getting in the middle of them! Pick them off one by one while staying outside their swarm, or use an attack with a large area of effect to clear them quickly.

Watch for ranged attackers like skeletons! You won't be able to get close without being hit, so use corners and cover to keep out of their line of sight, and use long-distance weapons of your own to clear them out.

Keep an eye out for emeralds and loot which enemies will drop when you defeat them. Even useless items can be sold!

Health bar about to hit zero? Minecraft Dungeons gives you three lives, so you can pick yourself up and try again from where you left off. After that, you'll have to redo the whole level from scratch!

Completely stuck? The game's areas are designed to be slightly different every time you play—so you may get luckier if you have to try again! Level layouts will shift, while enemies and treasure may be in different places. Even bosses will appear at different times!

DUNGEON SECRET

Don't worry if you find a new, more powerful weapon and you have to ditch your old one. Minecraft Dungeons is full of mighty armaments —chuck out the old ones and power up!

LEVELING UP

Earning new levels in Minecraft Dungeons is as simple as defeating enemies to gain XP—but there are some tricks to hitting the game's high levels faster.

LV **26**

You'll want to level up fast in the game to take on some of its tougher challenges. And after beating the whole game once, you'll need to keep leveling to take on two much harder difficulty versions of every mission!

Leveling up also grants you enchantment points to plug into your gear and unlock powerful bonuses (more on those on the next page).

LEVEL
2

POWER
1

SELECT ENCHANTMENT

You can choose from randomized enchantments for every item. Select one now.

As you might expect, easier enemies will grant you lower amounts of XP for defeating them than bosses—but bosses are tough and time-consuming to repeat. So if you're serious about leveling up as quickly as possible, seek out areas with lots of weak enemies you can defeat again and again.

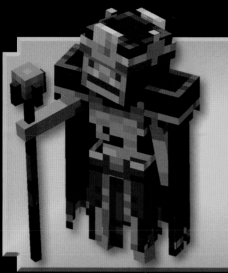

MOB RULE!

There are a few spots where enemies will appear endlessly, letting you farm XP quickly. The Necromancer enemies in the Desert Temple mission are one example of this, though the best area to harvest XP is in the Redstone Mines, where you'll find mob spawners that spit out enemies continuously.

Don't worry too much about grinding toward new levels. For your first run through the game, you should move up levels roughly at the same rate as you unlock new areas. Whenever you start a new area, you can also tune its difficulty up or down a little based on your current power level if you're finding progress a little difficult—or too easy!

LEVEL UP!

Enchantment point earned

While Minecraft Dungeons does not cap players at any particular top level, the game's Achievements and Trophy list only rewards you for hitting Level 50.

ENCHANTING EQUIPMENT

Enchanting lets you add powerful magical abilities to most of your equipment which can work in combination to provide powerful bonuses.

Every piece of armor, melee weapon, and bow in Minecraft Dungeons can be given extra abilities through enchanting, with better gear sometimes having two or even three enchantment slots per item.

You can examine which enchantments an item can receive via your inventory. To begin with, many items you find will have just a single enchantment slot, which you can fill with one of up to four enchantments options.

Don't see an enchantment option you like? Most gear can be found quite easily in the game, so if there's nothing you can see yourself using, it may be worth waiting to spend your enchantment points on something else, or until you find a different version of the same item with better enchantment possibilities.

32 RARE

CLAYMORE

88-157 melee damage

Powerful Pushback

A massive sword that seems impossibly heavy to lift yet rests easily in a just warrior's hands.

POWER   SPEED   AREA

Enchantments

Artifacts fact! Unlike your other gear, artifacts cannot be enchanted. They're powerful enough already, thank you very much.

You can make enchantments more powerful by spending further points to level up their effects. Higher enchantment levels require more enchantment points, however, so to begin with it's best not to spend them all in the same place.

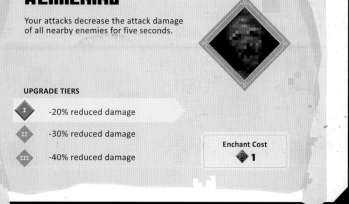

WEAKENING

Your attacks decrease the attack damage of all nearby enemies for five seconds.

UPGRADE TIERS

I   -20% reduced damage
II -30% reduced damage
III -40% reduced damage

Enchant Cost
1

REUSE AND RECYCLE!

Outgrown a piece of gear or found a better version? You can get your enchantment points back by dismantling any enchanted item, which rewards you with Emerald currency and returns any enchantment points so you can spend them on something else.

To start off with, we recommend enchantments which make enemies a little easier to handle, such as Weakening (reduced damage) or Freezing (reduced speed). When you're enchanting your bow, look for the powerful Supercharged (increased damage) or Infinity (which returns arrows to your quiver).

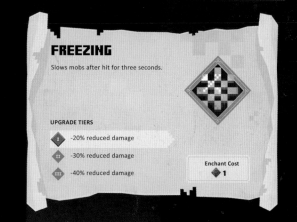

FREEZING

Slows mobs after hit for three seconds.

UPGRADE TIERS

I   -20% reduced damage
II -30% reduced damage
III -40% reduced damage

Enchant Cost
1

Minecraft Dungeons has dozens of enchantments to experiment with, so you're sure to find combinations which fit your particular play style!

PLAYING WITH FRIENDS

Minecraft Dungeons is a lot of fun as a solo adventure—but it's even better with friends!

The whole game can be played with other players by your side, up to four players overall. These players can either be local—all playing on the same console (perhaps all squeezed on the same sofa!)—or online.

Levels will adjust their difficulty depending on how many people are playing. The more players you have with you, the more enemies will appear. In other words, twice as many players does not mean you'll beat the same level twice as fast!

LOOT FOR ALL!

When playing in multiplayer, treasure items are reserved for individual players—so one person cannot go around and scoop up all the goodies, leaving you without any rewards for all your hard work.

To set up a multiplayer game with those on the same console, make sure you select "Offline Game" on the character select screen. Then simply connect the number of controllers you need and proceed.

To set up an online multiplayer game, select "Online Game." You can then invite friends, or wait for them to see you and join via their games. To join an online multiplayer game set up by someone else, head to your friends menu and hit "Join" there.

When playing online, you'll only be able to join the games of people you know already who are your friends on that particular console (or via Xbox Live if playing on PC). There is no matchmaking service for finding other players, so you'll always know who you're playing with (and that they'll be helpful)!

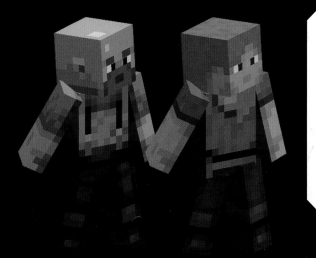

It's also worth remembering that online play may require access to that platform's online subscription service— Xbox Live on Xbox, PlayStation Plus on PlayStation, or Nintendo Switch Online on Nintendo Switch. If you don't have a subscription already, speak to a parent or whoever pays your console's bills!

CAMPSITE COMPANIONS

The campsite is your home in Minecraft Dungeons. Here's your camp-lete guide to what's on offer!

Complete the very quick Squid Coast tutorial and you'll arrive at your campsite—it's actually the area you find at the very end of the mission! But there's not much here, yet...

Over time, you'll find a variety of merchants will set up shop. These friendly villagers will sell you new gear and polish up items you already own, among other things.

Need somewhere to practice with your chosen weapons and armor? Head south and you'll find a pair of test dummies, ready and waiting for you to test out your gear. (Honestly, they won't mind.)

Explore the area further and you'll find a house which fills with souvenirs as you progress further through the game. There's a couple of nice fires to sit by—but this is no time to relax!

MISSING A NEIGHBOR?

Don't worry if a shopkeeper isn't in your campsite to start with—just keep progressing through the game's story and you'll find the area growing in things to do as you return here after each mission.

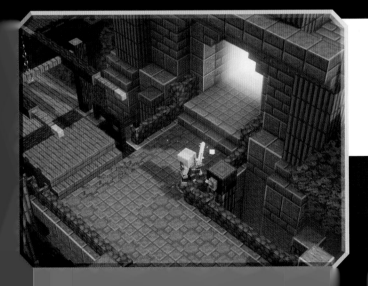

Head to the bottom right of your campsite to find a temple beyond a drawbridge—though you won't be able to access this until you beat the game...

Ready to head out, adventurer?
Let's get started!

CREEPER WOODS

With your campsite set up, it's time for your first proper mission in Creeper Woods...

This dark forest area is where you'll find a caravan of captured villagers who need rescuing from the forces of the Arch-Illager. Unfortunately, it's also where you'll find a horde of familiar-looking enemies.

Creeper Woods introduces many of the basic enemy types you'll find in the game. There are zombies (slow moving, but like to attack in big groups), skeleton archers (which fire arrows from range), and Creepers (they're a blast!), which act as any Minecraft fan might expect ... they go bang!

There are also Vindicators, who are corrupted Illagers wielding axes, and Enchanters, red-robed Illagers who will use magic to make other enemies stronger.

When facing an enemy made more powerful by an Enchanter, attacking the Enchanter first will make the other enemy vulnerable again!

WORLDWIDE WEBS!

Midway through this area you'll find a cave area with spiders. These enemies will attack you from range with their webs. If hit, you'll be trapped in place until you break yourself free, so avoid their projectiles if possible.

Finally, you'll come to an area full of caravans where the villager prisoners are being held. You'll need to free five captives, each marked on your screen with yellow arrows. Simply approach each prisoner and you'll get the prompt to tap a button and free them.

After that, it's just a short walk north to the level's exit.

SOGGY SWAMP

This waterlogged level is a spooky marsh full of poisonous water, where witches throw burning potions. Careful where you step...

You're here to put a stop to the evil witches' potion brewing, which first means destroying their potion equipment. Simply follow the level—steering clear of the toxic green water! You'll eventually find yourself in an area with five small cauldrons.

Destroy these bubbling potions one by one and clear out the enemies nearby, and you'll have completed your first objective.

Watch out for witches, who throw potions of burning pink flames at your feet. If you're caught in the flames, make sure to move quickly to avoid taking damage!

YOU AND OOZE ARMY?!

Other new enemies here include baby zombies, who will rush at you fast, and giant green slimes, which split into smaller slimes after being attacked.

After destroying the potions, you'll find yourself in a cave area with the game's first miniboss—the Enderman. Minecraft fans will know these terrifying enemies like to teleport away after taking damage, then pop up right behind you! Use arrows to take down this dangerous foe from afar.

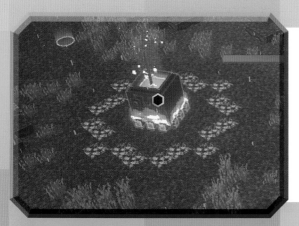

Once you're through the cave, it's only a little farther until Soggy Swamp's boss ... the Corrupted Cauldron. This gigantic pot of potion needs to be destroyed, and it'll continually spawn smaller enemies and slimes until you take it down.

With the cauldron smashed, the Arch-Illager's potion supply is gone. Phew! But there's still plenty to do...

PUMPKIN PASTURES

This autumnal area is one of the game's more straightforward levels, but you'll still need your wits about you to raise the alarm and save a village!

Your mission is to find the last place in Pumpkin Pastures still standing—and warn its inhabitants of the coming Illager threat. This means fighting your way through a long stretch of woods, dotted with burned houses. These are the villages which have already been pillaged!

About halfway through you'll find a castle where the Arch-Illager will ambush you, spawning more of the same enemies you've battled previously. You'll then need to hit two switches to lower the castle's drawbridge and progress farther.

You'll face a mix of familiar enemies here so there won't be too many nasty surprises. Just keep following the game's yellow direction arrow —there are no major puzzles to navigate.

After this, you're back on the trail to find that village! Progress a little farther and you'll find the level's big threat—a boss named the Evoker.

EVOKER OUTRAGE!

The Evoker has some serious magic powers, and is able to conjure sets of fangs which can deal a lot of damage to you. He can also summon Vexes, flying enemies who will fly over and attack you separately. Keep an eye on the patterns of his attacks—when and where the fangs appear —and keep your distance if possible. Use ranged attacks like arrows to finish him off!

Finally, you'll find the village you've been looking for all this time. Head to the middle, to the town bell, and ring it. Level complete! Oh, no, wait ... there are a few more enemies needing defeating first. Get rid of these— including another round with the Evoker—and you're finally done.

Enter the Town Hall building to the right of the square to complete the level. Congratulations—you have warned the village! But there's plenty more evil to get rid of before you can celebrate properly...

CACTI CANYON

You'll need to fight your way through this arid area full of desert husks and canyon-dwelling undead to reach the Desert Temple. It's hot stuff!

As the level begins, you're asked to power the nearby beacon. Simply walk over and flip its switch to unlock a way forward. Follow the usual yellow marker to your next objective and you'll eventually find yourself with five more beacons to power on.

Activate [A]

It's here things get trickier, as Cacti Canyon's narrow paths and deep ravines open up into a wider area. Enemies can come at you from all sides and quickly outnumber you—so it's worth brushing up on all of the new types you'll find here.

READY TO ROCK!

Husks are desert versions of zombies with beefier defenses, meaning they will take longer to take down. You'll also meet Geomancers: rock-summoning Illagers who can try to trap you by conjuring up pillars to block your path—some of which even explode!

Take particular care in the desert to avoid the steep drops, and prioritize taking out any Geomancers if you see rock columns forming around you (they often hide farther away, and attack you from afar).

With the five beacons taken care of, you'll need to press on a little farther to find yourself at a locked gate, where the Arch-Illager will ambush you by summoning several waves of mobs. Defeat these, and the gate will lower so you can pick up a blue key golem.

Use the blue key golem on the nearby blue gate, and follow this path until you can pick up the golden key which will unlock the level's final short section. Passing through the golden gate you'll need to fight off one final Arch-Illager ambush—this one a little longer—before reaching the Desert Temple. Head to the door, and you'll have beaten the level!

Unlock A

DESERT TEMPLE

This sandy shrine is supposed to be the final resting place for an undead army. Better get there before the Arch-Illager claims it for himself...

The mission begins with a command to find the tomb of the undead Necromancer—someone who can raise an army of the dead! You'll encounter a couple of new enemies here: the ghostly Wraith, which conjures up an area of hazardous blue flames, and the Necromancer, a creepy magical being with a staff that summons a whole crowd of basic enemies, like zombies and skeletons.

Head forward through the dungeon following the yellow marker until you reach a locked door, and a golden keyhole. From here, you'll need to venture off to one side through a series of small rooms to locate the golden key. Grab that and bring it back to the keyhole, and it's back to finding the tomb again!

Continue on and you'll face a couple of tougher fights against an Enderman—but you've dealt with this enemy before. Push forward, surviving another ambush from the Arch-Illager, and you'll eventually reach the tomb itself.

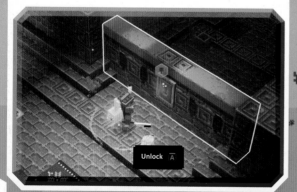

Unlock A

Awaken Ⓐ

Here, you're told to simply fetch a staff—the magical artifact used to conjure the army of the undead. Surely it can't be that simple? You guessed it—claiming the staff also woke its former owner, the Nameless One. He's a super-sized version of a Necromancer!

CROWNING ACHIEVEMENT!

The Nameless One will create hordes of smaller enemies for you to fight, but it's the green magic orbs he fires from his staff you really need to worry about. Keep moving and dodge to avoid getting hit by these. This boss can also create mirror images of himself to confuse you into attacking the wrong one—but you'll know which is real as only the actual boss will take damage when attacked.

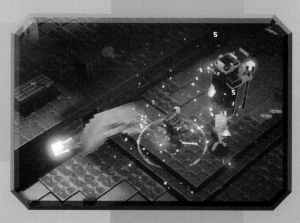

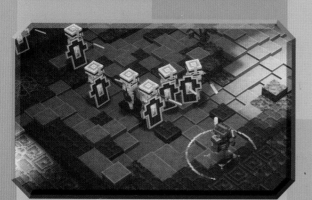

Prevail in your fight with the Nameless One and you'll be able to head through the unlocked door to the level's end, with its undead army hopefully gone for good...

REDSTONE MINES

Beneath a snowy mountain range lies a vast fiery mine, filled with lava and out-of-control minecarts. Sounds like a fun day out!

Your first job here is to find and free a trio of villagers being made to work within the mine. But to get to them, you'll have to fight through plenty of enemies first. Keep an eye out for spawners: magical metal crates which create waves of enemies whenever you get close.

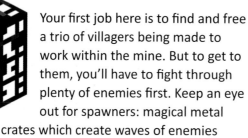

Redstone Mines is also home to green cave spiders (faster, poisonous versions of their bigger spider brothers) and Illagers armed with heavy crossbows that deal an increased amount of damage.

But it's not just enemies you'll need to watch out for. The whole mine is criss-crossed by minecart tracks, which minecarts whiz along at great speed. If you're standing in the way of one (and it's easy to get distracted) it'll take off a huge chunk of your health. On the upside, if an enemy is standing in the way, they'll be damaged instead!

Progress through the level until you reach a wide area where you're told to free villagers—there are three in this first section. Simply head over to them and you'll be able to set them free (while dodging enemy arrows, of course).

Continue on and you'll likely find yourself facing another Evoker or two—remember to avoid their fang attack as much as possible. Next you'll need to free more villagers—there are six in this second section. Finally, you'll be told to leave the mine. But, of course, things are never so simple...

SEEING RED!

The redstone golem is one of Minecraft Dungeons' toughest enemies—and you'll fight it here on its home turf. It will chase you, try to knock you into lava, summon exploding rocks to block your path— and you'll need to avoid all this while navigating narrow and hazardous surroundings.

Once you have beaten the redstone golem, the level's exit can be found directly after.

FIERY FORGE

Things are really heating up! This underground forge is where the game's molten golems are made—ready to put them out?

You'll begin just outside the forge itself, on a snowy mountainside with simple enemies to get past. The forge's main entrance is well guarded, so you're headed in a side door. Just before you do, look to one side and a small path leading away: there's a secret chest hidden here.

Once in the mine, you'll be asked to find the forge cores which run this evil power plant. While the enemies here are familiar, you'll also have to face multiple redstone golems! Yes, smaller versions of the last level's boss are just stomping around here, fresh out of the forge's ovens. This time around, at least, you have more room to maneuver.

Move forward until you reach a large area of networked forges, and are told to overload their cores. There are eight in total, and each will send out a shockwave of fire when they detonate. Avoid this blast—and also use it to your advantage to clear out any enemies caught in the way.

This particular area can be a real maze, so use the in-game map to track which cores you have yet to activate.

With all eight cores overloaded, it's time to make your escape. Continue on until the path narrows, and you reach this level's final boss fight. After several regular redstone golems, it's time to meet their bigger brother, The Monstrosity.

LAVA GOOD FIGHT?

The Monstrosity packs tougher versions of the regular redstone golem attacks—so be sure to keep your distance from its shockwave. Just like the redstone golem boss fight, there's plenty of fire around to get knocked into. It will also sometimes spit lava as well—which, honestly, is just bad manners.

The other thing to watch out for are the redstone cubes which spawn. These red blocks look a little like dice, and will tumble around after you. Defeat them as quickly as possible (you can set off more cores here with shockwaves that wipe them out quickly) and then concentrate on the big boss when you can.

Once The Monstrosity has been smashed to rubble, head through the newly-opened gate and past a few remaining enemies to a mining lift, which is your way of exiting the level.

HIGHBLOCK HALLS

You've beaten the Arch-Illager's many minions—now it's time to take the fight directly to him, within his own castle!

Highblock Halls is a huge location, so this final showdown is actually split over two levels. For now, you're tasked with reaching the Arch-Illager's throne room, which means taking on his most elite (and angriest) soldiers.

The Royal Guard Illagers you meet here carry a large shield and won't take regular damage until it has been taken care of first. Explosive or firework arrows work well against them, as they typically bunch close together.

Continue through the castle's corridors until you reach a door which requires a golden key. Beware! As soon as you pick up the key golem, new enemies will spawn to make your way back to the door harder. Alternatively, this section can see the Arch-Illager simply spawn a mass of enemies to take down, without a key required.

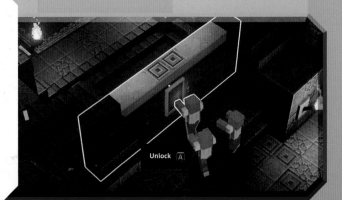

You'll now find yourself outside, with a slightly easier set of enemies to take care of. Clear these zombies and skeletons and have a breather ... and you may notice something odd about that wishing well. This is the secret entrance into the Arch-Illager's keep!

Head through the secret passage to emerge in the castle's kitchens. Here, you're asked to destroy the buffet on offer for the Arch-Illager's many troops. Don't let the Illager chefs wearing white hats stop you! You'll need to smash up three sets of buffet tables to progress.

Finally, you'll find yourself in the Arch-Illager's throne room—but he's going to throw everything else at you first before fighting you one-on-one.

So begins this level's final fight, featuring wave upon wave of Royal Guards, mixed with other Illagers, Enchanters, and Wraiths. As ever, use the space open to you to pick off enemies slowly, drawing them away from others. Make sure you get rid of magical enemies first, before Enchanters can buff other foes and Wraiths have time to set the level on fire.

With the throne room cleared, you're left to chase the Arch-Illager onto the castle battlements, and into the game's final level...

OBSIDIAN PINNACLE

This is it—your final showdown with the Arch-Illager and an end to his evil plans, once and for all!

Picking up the action directly from where the previous level left off, Obsidian Pinnacle begins high up on the castle battlements. You'll need to clear many of the same enemies here as in Highblock Halls, including the tough Royal Guards, but now in much narrower areas.

Use the area's jump pads to move forward and you'll eventually come to a magical fence with another ambush of enemies, then a section with two beacons to power on either side. Hit these two switches and move forward.

This next area, covered in areas of lava, is home to several redstone golems. You didn't think the game would end without bringing these guys back again, did you? Defeat them as before, focusing on one at a time. Explore more of the level's side-passages here and you may find a third!

Head inside the castle and you'll find yourself in a series of hallways which open on a large banquet hall. There's a secret area here you'll be able to see if you open your in-game map—check one of the bookshelves for a switch to open a hidden door with treasure inside and a mysterious rune ... (more on those later!)

Back outside the castle, you'll find yourself climbing higher and higher. Defeat one last redstone golem and you'll reach a steep set of stone stairs. Get ready—this is the game's final boss fight!

The Arch-Illager here has two phases—and to start off with, he's actually not too difficult. Just stay back from him and target his tiny body with arrows while dodging the purple projectiles he fires toward you and the Illagers he will sometimes spawn.

But even when you think the Arch-Illager is defeated ... something worse is to come.

HEARTBREAKER!

The game's real final boss is named the Heart of Ender, a much tougher enemy. Again, the idea is to avoid its purple magic attacks while hitting it at range. Having trouble? Check out this book's boss section for a full and in-depth guide!

With both the Arch-Illager and Heart of Ender defeated, you have beaten the game! Follow the magic trail to discover what has become of the Arch-Illager and enjoy a final cut-scene.

CREEPY CRYPT

Some levels in Minecraft Dungeons hold a secret, second area to unlock! Here's how to find and explore them all...

If you go down to Creeper Woods today, you're in for a big surprise! And that surprise is called Creepy Crypt, a big new dungeon you can explore separately, accessible via your campsite map.

Like every secret level, Creepy Crypt is almost completely random. Every time you play, the layout will have shifted! This means you can explore it as many times as you like and always find something new.

WOULD YOU LOOT AT THAT!

Secret levels hold no major bosses or puzzles—they're primarily designed to be areas you can farm enemies for loot and Emeralds.

Creepy Crypt is very simple to unlock. Head left as you start Creeper Woods, and you'll eventually find a building with a redstone switch. Hit that switch and enter to find a map for Creepy Crypt on the table. Every secret level requires you to find a map to it first, but after that it can be accessed from your campsite map table.

Once in Creepy Crypt, the level will direct you to find a lost tomb hidden somewhere in the dungeon. That is the only requirement—just find it and then the exit, and grab lots of loot along the way!

Enemies here are the lower level mobs you might find in Creeper Woods. Keep an eye out for big tomb lids you can move to find treasure, and make sure you use your map to explore every passage the level conjures up to get as much loot as possible.

SOGGY CAVE

As you might expect from its name, Soggy Cave is Soggy Swamp's secret level. You'd better put on your waterproof boots...

When exploring Soggy Swamp, be on the lookout for a second cave after the first you must pass through (where you fight the Enderman), around halfway into the level. Once inside, activate the beacon and defeat the mobs to summon the Soggy Cave map.

Keep it secret, keep it safe! Some secret levels are so secret, the method to unlock them may not always appear. You may need to explore Soggy Swamp several times before this second cave pops up.

Load up Soggy Cave from your campsite map and you'll find it's a very small place. Your only job here is to find and explore its ruins, then hop back onto your boat at the end.

Push A

It's impossible to get lost, though you'll need to fiddle with a couple of redstone switches which block your path. (If you're stuck, the answer is usually to hit the switches in the following order: left, right, left, right, left.)

Enemies here include witches and slimes, just like you'd find in the main Soggy Swamp. It's worth noting this area can also drop some nice armor—including the Evocation Robe, which boosts your speed.

You'll likely be able to explore all of this level in just a few minutes—after which, it's time to head out and back to dry land.

41

ARCH HAVEN

By far the most difficult secret area to unlock, this moonlit village is tough to find!

Arch Haven's map is hidden in a pirate ship within Pumpkin Pastures, but this ship only has a rare chance of appearing. You'll likely need to search the level multiple times to see when it shows up.

The best way to find the pirate ship is to use your map to check through all branching paths at the beginning of the Pumpkin Pastures level, then to head back to camp and reload if the ship is not there.

Travel A

Once found, Arch Haven is a simple area which asks you to defeat enemies to open up your path forward, then collect three spellbooks dotted around town.

Keep following your arrow until you're back on your pirate ship, ready to sail into the sunset.

Grab A

LOWER TEMPLE

Buried under the sands of the Desert Temple, more monsters and treasure await beneath...

You can unlock the Lower Temple within the main Desert Temple level, just after you use your gold key. Explore the side room found right after, and power on its beacons to create a bridge over to the Lower Temple's map.

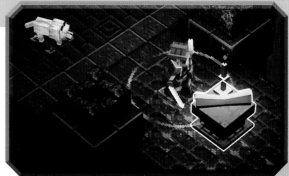

Travel to the Lower Temple from your campsite map to find another area full of swinging axe traps, powerful Necromancers and fiery Wraiths. There are plenty of passages to explore for loot, so use your map to make sure you've checked every path and corner.

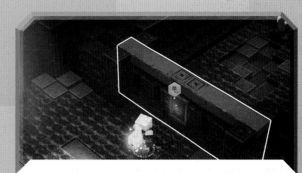

Several Necromancers can spawn at once, making for some tricky fights in tight surroundings. Make sure to take these enemies out first to stop them conjuring up more!

Follow your arrow, and you'll eventually come to a locked gate needing a golden key nearby. Track this down and you'll be able to move on towards the level's exit.

UNDERHALLS

One of the game's tougher secret levels, Underhalls is at least easy to find. Dust off your best suit of armor for another trip to Highblock Keep...

You can unlock the Underhalls mission from a secret area close to the beginning of Highblock Keep. From the start of that level, just follow the opening corridor until you see a staircase with two shields to either side. Hit the blue shield to open up a room containing the Underhalls map. Easy!

Grab and run! Once you've unlocked a secret level's map, you can head straight back to your campsite to load it up. There's no need to continue on with the rest of the level!

As you might expect from an area similar to Highblock Castle, the secret Underhalls level contains many of the same tough enemies. Be on the lookout for the Royal Guard Illagers and the fiery Wraiths as you explore its passageways.

The Underhalls level begins in a cellar underneath the castle. It's a huge area, and you'll need to find a blue key golem somewhere within it all to progress. Just follow the golden arrow and you'll be guided in its general direction.

Once you've unlocked the key golem gate, your mission is to simply explore the level further until you find its final exit. Be sure to use your in-game map to keep track of where you've been and which areas might still hold treasure in this dark labyrinth.

RUNE HUNTING

The game's final secret level is a little different, and requires a lot of extra work. Remember that rune you found?

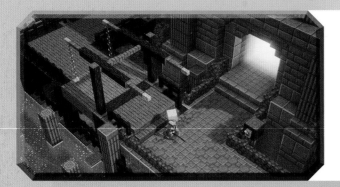

Once you have beaten the game, you will be able to access the temple within your campsite. Leap over to it using the new jump pads on the far right. Make sure you hit the switch to lower the drawbridge—this will make your next visit a lot easier!

Inside, you'll find some intriguing pictures—just who are these strange looking folk? Head to the altar to place one hidden rune from each of the game's levels and unlock that final secret area.

HOUNDED OUT!

Perhaps you've found a rune or two already while adventuring? If you've only got a couple left, you can examine this portrait of a dog to get a clue to the levels you still need to search.

Creeper Woods

In the section where you free five villagers, head to the lower left part of this area to find a set of mysterious blocks. Hit the switch to open up a doorway to the rune location.

Pumpkin Pastures

While finding the village, you'll pass a large castle. Head to the right of the wall to find a switch behind a set of crates.

Soggy Swamp

At the end of the level, after defeating the Cauldron, you'll find a switch to the right of the exit behind some mushrooms. Tasty!

Cacti Canyon

In the location where you find the blue key golem, the switch to unlock the rune area is to the right behind a palm tree.

Redstone Mines

You'll find the rune location here in the section you must free six villagers. Head north, to a hidden switch behind a clump of redstone blocks.

Desert Temple

After picking up the golden key golem, look behind a desert shrub in the next room. Hit the switch and enter the room it unlocks for the rune.

Fiery Forge

At the beginning of the level, look to one side as you enter the mine, by a crushed redstone golem. The switch is hidden on the wall behind it.

Highblock Halls

Remember the outside area where it rained? Head there to find a stone switch on the northern wall.

Obsidian Pinnacle—We called out this rune in our guide for the level, so you may have it already! In case you missed it, you'll need to hit a switch in the castle's library.

MOOSHROOM MISSION

Collected all those runes? Plug them into the temple altar and you'll open up one final secret mission on your campsite map...

Look to the top right of the map, to find a curious mission named only "???". Wondering what's in store? We'd better get a "moove" on—it's well "pasture" time we explored further!

This secret mooshroom level is filled with ... well, mooshrooms! Minecraft's odd mix of cow and mushroom can only be found here, hiding away in this "amoosing" level. While they might appear friendly, we've "herd" this creature will attack on sight.

There are a few chests to pick up, but otherwise there's very little to do here aside from simply having a look at it all—and taking on a very special boss. Remember the Redstone Monstrosity? Well, it turns out there's a Mooshroom variant.

DAIRY DEMON!

The Mooshroom Monstrosity can be found waiting at the very end of this level. Take it on just as you did the regular Monstrosity, but beware this version's added ability to summon regular Mooshrooms and also spit flaming projectiles.

Beat the Mooshroom Monstrosity and you'll complete the level, ending its "beef" with you forever. (Worried we'd "milk" the cow puns too much? You were "udderly" right.)

49

FRIENDLY CHARACTERS

Not everyone in Minecraft Dungeons is out to get you! These amiable allies will lend you a helping hand, leg, or trotter...

MERCHANTS AND TRADERS

The Village Merchant sells common and rare items for Emeralds, while the Luxury Merchant sells higher rarity items. Alternatively, head to the hooded Mystery Merchant to gamble your money on something random. The Blacksmith lets you upgrade items to a higher rarity, and asks you complete three missions in exchange. The Gift Wrapper, meanwhile, lets you share your items with other players in your party while at your campsite.

Some items are otherwise very hard to find, so it's well worth tossing a few coins to the helpful merchants—you never know what you might get in exchange! Just make sure you equip your best loot before chatting to them. The gear they provide is tailored to your current level.

KEY GOLEM

Well, locky here! Key golems are a … key ally you'll need to beat many of Minecraft Dungeons' levels. If you ever find yourself at a locked door, you'll know one of these little creatures are hiding nearby. Golems come in both blue and gold varieties, and you may need to find one color to then unlock a second door with the other. Just make sure to protect them once you pick them up! If they get hit, they'll try to run away back into hiding.

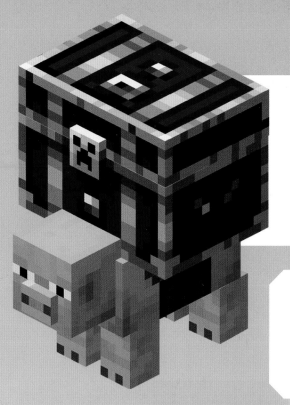

TREASURE PIG

We've heard of a piggy bank—but never one that's able to run around on its own! These loot-laden creatures can be found in many Minecraft Dungeon levels, though they won't give up their goodies willingly.

It's up to you—do you leave the Treasure Pigs as they are? Or do you want the emeralds and items they carry in their treasure chests? If it's the latter option, you'll need to pork chop...

VILLAGERS

The Arch-Illager has captured many villagers to use in his nefarious schemes. You'll need to save many of these harmless inhabitants over the course of your adventure, so always keep a lookout for anyone needing help.

COWS AND SHEEP

Familiar from the main Minecraft game, these friendly farmyard animals can be found across many of the woods and grasslands you explore. Just like in Minecraft, they will drop food items that you can eat to restore health.

PETS GALORE

Meet Minecraft Dungeons' menagerie of faithful, furry, and flappy friends. Which will you take into battle?

WOLF

The friendly wolf can be summoned to your side using the Tasty Bone artifact, a common item you'll be able to find early on in Creeper Woods. With this artifact equipped, you will be able to spawn your furry friend once every 30 seconds and watch as he takes down any enemies within nearby sight. Good boy!

LLAMA

Want to cause some drama? Summon the llama! You'll need the Tasty Wheat artifact found in Cacti Canyon. Just like in real life, this funky-looking creature will spit at anything it decides is an enemy! These guys are useful if you're focusing on mainly dealing ranged damage.

Down but not out! All summonable pets can perish if they take too many hits, but your artifact will let you bring them back as soon as it has finished its cooldown.

BAT

Getting in a flap? Meet the bat! These airborne allies are the only pet not to be summoned with an artifact. Instead, you'll need the common Spelunker Armor, which can also be found in Cacti Canyon. Bats act as a handy distraction when facing hordes of foes, and will swoop over to deal small amounts of damage to any enemy close by.

IRON GOLEM

The hulking iron golem is hugely powerful, although you'll need the rare Golem Kit artifact to summon one. The Golem Kit is normally only found when playing on the game's top Apocalypse difficulty, but you can also try your luck for one at the campsite's Wandering Trader. Not only can they deal massive damage to nearby enemies, they can also take plenty of it too.

COSMETIC CREATURES!

If you own the Hero Edition of Minecraft Dungeons, you'll be able to equip a bonus baby chicken pet which is purely for show. This friendly creature won't attack, but will always follow you around—even in your campsite.

EVERY ENEMY EXAMINED

Minecraft's bad guys are all here—and they brought some backup! Here's every enemy you'll face...

ZOMBIE

These familiar, slow-moving enemies are your basic Minecraft mob. Easy to defeat, they're less fun in crowds (and even less fun at parties).

SKELETON

Make no bones about it, these arrow-wielding enemies can be a pain if you don't take them out quickly. Fire an arrow back to send them home to the grave.

SPIDER

These pesky arachnids are even more annoying in Minecraft Dungeons. Not only can they shoot webs at you from a distance, they can also now stick you to the floor until you break free!

CREEPER

Minecraft's most memorable enemy returns in explosive style. Defeat it quickly to stop its fuse, or let it detonate to take out other enemies nearby!

SLIME

This resident of Soggy Swamp will put you in a sticky situation. Just like in the regular Minecraft, it'll split itself several times before being fully defeated.

CAVE SPIDER

Like a spider, but meaner. Hey, you'd probably have a bad attitude if you were forced to live in a cave as well.

HUSK

These desert-dwelling zombies have adapted to their tough surroundings by building up their health and attack power. Clearly they've been working out.

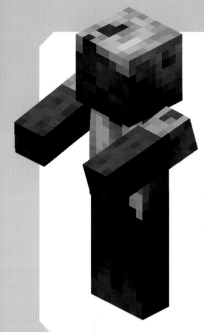

BABY ZOMBIE

Don't be fooled by their cute size! These little zombie tykes are quick on their feet and motivated by an adorable desire to see you defeated.

CHICKEN JOCKEY

A rare baby zombie who rides a chicken. Very rarely, you might find a chicken jockey tower, a stack of baby zombies on top of one another!

VINDICATOR

This is your basic angry Illager, though he probably wouldn't describe himself like that. Look out for a less-basic armored version, too.

ENCHANTER

This red-robed magician won't attack you itself, but it will buff nearby enemies to make them more powerful. Wand-er who you should attack first?

PILLAGER

What do you call an Illager with a crossbow? A Pillager, apparently. Tougher versions of this enemy with heftier bows are known as Fanatics.

GEOMANCER

This magic-wielding Illager summons stone pillars from the ground to surround you, including an explosive totem that looks like a creeper!

ROYAL GUARD

An elite Illager armed with a mace and enormous shield. Loyal to the Arch-Illager, you'll find these top troops only in his castle.

WITCH

Another Soggy Swamp resident, the Witch will throw poisonous potions at you and healing potions at itself. Unfortunately, it never gets the two confused.

WRAITH

A ghost-like demon which summons blue fire and can teleport where you least expect it. Good at hide-and-seek.

ENDERMAN

Don't look it in the eye! This totally creepy enemy pops up several times as a monstrous mini-boss, dotted within certain levels.

SUMMONER

These tough mini-bosses are all about summoning other enemies to do their evil bidding, and nothing about mathematical sums.

SKELETON VANGUARD

Suited-up skeletons, these enemies are immune until you get rid of their shield first.

CONJURED SLIME

A purple slime and friend to the Corrupted Cauldron boss, this enemy likes to shoot purple projectiles at you.

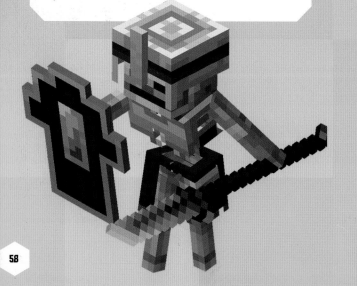

REDSTONE CUBE

Summoned into battle by the Redstone Monstrosity, these red cubes look almost like a set of dice—but you shouldn't try to take any chances with them.

SKELETON HORSEMEN

An uncommon mini-boss, this troupe of mounted skeleton cavalry ride skeleton horses. If you pick them off one at a time, then they won't be around "furlong."

VEX

Conjured up by an Evoker, these winged ghosts might look cute if they didn't wield an extremely sharp sword.

MOOSHROOM

Is it a mushroom or is it a cow? Either way, this huffy heifer wants to hurt you. But where in Minecraft Dungeons might they be hiding?

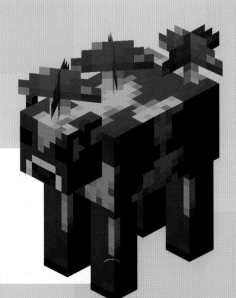

EVERY BOSS BEATEN

Powerful boss enemies lurk at the end of most levels—heed our advice on how to defeat them before it's too late!

EVOKER

This tricksy Illager is the first boss you'll face in Minecraft Dungeons, and one you'll want to get the hang of quickly. After his first appearance in Pumpkin Pastures, he will regularly pop up throughout the rest of the game!

The Evoker has a couple of nasty fang attacks which spread spiked teeth along the ground. Whenever you see these unfolding, it's important to run (or use your dodge roll) to get out of the way as soon as possible. Stand close to the Evoker and the fangs will form a circle around you. Stand farther away, and the fangs will form a straight line toward your position.

The Evoker can also spawn a flock of four Vexes, ghostly flying enemies who will fly quickly toward you and try to attack. These should be dealt with as soon as they appear, as you won't be able to run away from them. Our advice is to deal with Evoker from range, using arrows to take down Vexes and any special arrow types (like firework arrows) on the Evoker himself.

CORRUPTED CAULDRON

This unusual boss isn't alive, though it is enchanted with evil magic which spawns other enemies and spits purple fire!

You'll find the Corrupted Cauldron at the end of the Soggy Swamp level—the only place it will appear. Your goal is to smash it as quickly as possible, as it won't stop filling the screen with other enemies until you do. We'd recommend avoiding the purple slimes it creates as much as possible and steering clear of the cauldron itself, as it can conjure up purple fire around its base.

We found that it's possible to duck out of the area where the cauldron actually sits, back past the entrance where you came in. If you're taking too much damage it's worth popping in here to heal up—the enemies won't follow.

NAMELESS ONE

This creepy flying Necromancer is a souped-up version you'll only find in the Desert Temple level. It will attack you from range, sending green energy orbs in your direction at slow speed. You'll have plenty of time to avoid these, so keep moving!

If you're feeling lucky, these projectiles can be hit with a melee attack to send them flying back toward the Nameless One. It's a bit of a gamble, however—you'll need to get the timing just right to avoid being hit yourself.

The Nameless One will also raise skeleton vanguard enemies, shield-wielding undead you'll need to remove before they take damage. Deal with these as quickly as possible before returning to damage the boss.

Finally, the Nameless One can conjure mirror images of itself to disguise where it is hiding. You'll need to hit the real Nameless One to make all of its clones disappear.

REDSTONE GOLEM

This huge lump of animated redstone and rock is the boss of the Redstone Mines level, but it will later appear as a regular enemy in the game's tough final levels.

Your first fight against the Redstone Golem is by far the hardest, however, not helped by the area you battle it being filled with fiery lava pools.

The Redstone Golem has two attacks: it can swipe you with its long rocky arms if you get too close, or lay a series of explosive mines on the floor around itself that detonate if you step on top.

The key to defeating this monster is to deal as much melee damage as possible when it has paused to drop those mines, then quickly move out of its path when it begins moving again.

You can also shoot it with arrows while it is on the move—but it's important to also have an escape route planned! Do not get drawn into long chases—the more you move around this area, the more likely you are to find yourself surrounded by lava with nowhere else to go...

REDSTONE MONSTROSITY

The Redstone Golem's bigger brother, this enormous enemy is the final boss of Minecraft Dungeons' Fiery Forge.

Instead of mines, the Redstone Monstrosity has the power to summon endless supplies of redstone cubes, blocky enemies that will tumble around after you and pack a painful punch. It can also spray the area in front of it with a mouthful of fiery projectiles, and pummel you if you ever stand too close.

Make sure you keep on top of the Redstone Cubes as much as possible—they are impossible to avoid so will need to be dealt with before they deal damage to you. Use the interactive forges around the battle area to send shockwaves that will take them out, or slice them up with your melee weapon.

When you're not dealing with all that, you should use ranged attacks on the Monstrosity itself. We'd recommend firework arrows or the Corrupted Beacon artifact that summons a jet of powerful energy you can direct toward the boss. One good thing about the Monstrosity's size is that he moves slowly, so he is easy to target!

Finally, it's worth noting you can escape the boss fight area again here for a quick breather and to wait for your health potion to recharge. Good luck!

MOOSHROOM MONSTROSITY!

If you've unlocked the secret ??? Mooshroom level you'll face a second version of the Redstone Monstrosity which spawns mooshroom cows instead of redstone cubes, though the overall strategy to defeat it remains the same.

THE ARCH-ILLAGER

For all the trouble this guy causes over the course of the game, your final showdown with the Arch-Illager is surprisingly straightforward!

Watch out for his purple energy projectiles, which he'll fire toward you in horizontal waves. These spread out over a large radius but move slowly, meaning you can position yourself between them and avoid getting hit at all if you stand far enough back.

Unable to fight for himself, the Arch-Illager will instead rely on waves of other enemies he spawns to do his dirty work for him. Most of these won't cause you any issues, though look out for Vindicators and Redstone Golems which can occasionally be conjured up.

Use melee attacks on the spawned enemies and ranged attacks on the Arch-Illager and you'll soon have him beat. Unfortunately, the corrupted Orb of Dominance he wields isn't done with you yet...

... AND THE HEART OF ENDER

Minecraft Dungeon's final boss is an overpowered atrocity—a being of pure dark power formed by the Orb of Dominance to stop itself from being destroyed once and for all.

Looking like a spidery Enderman, this devastating demon will require you to stay on your toes at all times to avoid its lethal purple lasers.

The Heart of Ender will move around the area constantly, leaving trails of black fire behind it you'll need to avoid too. It can also summon multiple heads from the ground to fire even more lasers from their mouths.

The aim of the game here is to simply ensure you stay alive while chipping away at the Heart of Ender's overall health. Never allow yourself to get stuck inside one of its laser beams, or boxed into a corner.

Make sure you have plenty of arrows going into this final fight—and if all else fails and you do get stuck taking damage, remember you can always roll off the level to be teleported to safety (although with a bit of health taken as a penalty).

WEAPONS

Look sharp! With one of these weapons equipped you'll be well on your way to victory.

DAGGERS

A great weapon for your early adventuring, this pair of blades will quickly up your attack speed while letting you dual wield (which, let's be honest, just looks really cool).

DANCER'S SWORD

Speaking of speed, this rare unique weapon is among the speediest attack items in the game. If you can get your hands on one then you are on to a winning combo.

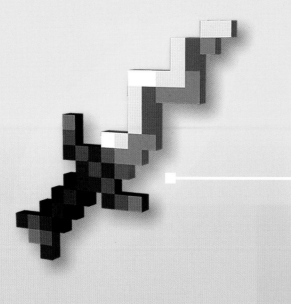

ETERNAL KNIFE

A weapon for soul-wielders, this hugely powerful blade makes up for what it lacks in speed and range with its immense strength. It can also gain souls and increases your general soul gathering.

AUTO CROSSBOW

The closest Minecraft Dungeons has to a machine gun, this ranged weapon increases its firing rate the longer you keep firing! Just be sure to keep an eye on your ammo reserves...

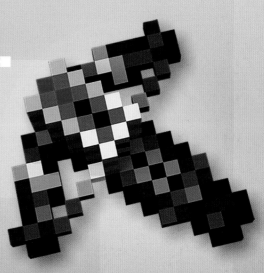

WHISPERING SPEAR

An elegant weapon for a more civilized time, this special spear has an abnormally long range, giving you the ability to strike from range without using a bow. Great for bosses where you might want to keep your distance.

ARMOR

Suit up! These top-tier armor sets will help you dress to impress and beat the rest.

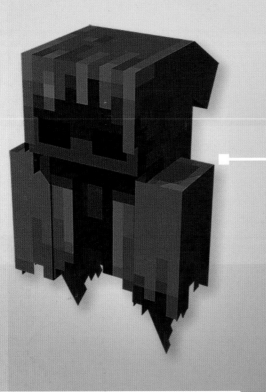

SOUL ROBE

This ghostly-looking gear boosts your artifact damage and lets you gain more souls. Its unique version, the much rarer Souldancer Robe, is even better as it can also sometimes completely save you from a particular attack.

SCALE MAIL

One of several easy-to-find armors available at the start of the game, this reduces the amount of damage you take while simultaneously boosting the damage you deal out. It's a good choice for an early character.

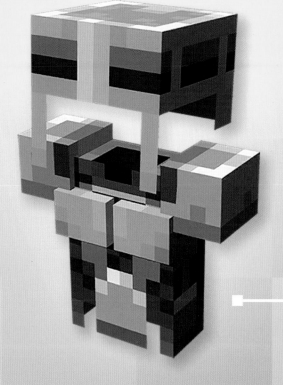

REINFORCED MAIL

A solid choice for melee fighters, this heavy-looking armor will heavily cut the amount of damage you take and has a chance to save you from particular attacks completely. The downside is your dodge roll speed is heavily impacted.

SPELUNKER ARMOR

This armor set and its unique variant, the Cave Crawler, lets you use a pet bat which is great for distracting enemies. It will also boost your health and give your damage a boost.

ARTIFACTS

Pack one of these powerful items in your pocket and you'll have the upper hand in any brawl! Professional dungeon players take note...

GONG OF WEAKENING

This super cymbal weakens any enemies around you—including bosses—by decreasing both their attack and defense. This means you can now get close to them and survive longer while under attack, while dealing huge amounts of damage to them!

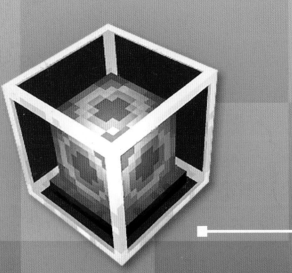

CORRUPTED BEACON

This powerful artifact should be a key item for any character using the game's souls mechanic. Its high-powered laser beam can sap the life out of most enemies and seriously damage bosses.

HARVESTER

Another must-have artifact for serious soul users, this item uses the souls you harvest to power a huge explosive effect. Summon the souls from that explosion and you're ready for another!

BOOTS OF SWIFTNESS

If you're looking to speed through missions quickly—especially while trying to find a specific secret or treasure—these boots are a necessity. You'll get a boost to your running speed so you can move quicker and become more nimble dodging enemy attacks.

GOLEM KIT

The Golem Kit—like any item which gives you a pet—can give you a huge boost, especially when playing solo. Not only do pets attack enemies, they can also draw fire and distract them, buying you valuable breathing room.

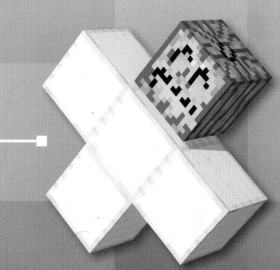

HOW TO MAKE MONEY ...FAST

Want to buy some better gear? Here's our guide to getting rich quick—no shady investments here, honest.

The game's emerald currency is fairly easy to come by, and you should quickly earn a stash by defeating tougher enemies, opening treasure chests, and smashing pots.

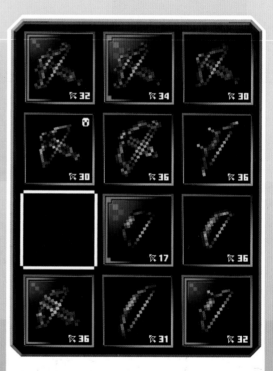

If you haven't fully explored the game's campsite area yet, now is a good time to do so. You'll find several hidden chests can pop up in different locations, including a rare ender chest which offers an even bigger payday.

Dedicated treasure hunters should keep on top of their inventory, and salvage any unwanted weapons, armor and artifacts for emeralds. You can do this at any point, not just at camp.

Minecraft Dungeons hands out new gear quickly, so you'll likely have a stash of items you no longer need. Keep an eye out for any item you get a better version of—there's no need to keep duplicates, so it's safe to dismantle the first.

If you're really serious about emerald hunting, you can use the Prospector enchantment on some items to increase your chances of finding emeralds from fallen enemies.

Tier 1 of the Prospector enchantment increases emerald drop chance by 100%, while Tiers 2 and 3 will give 200% and 300% respectively.

13 UNIQUE

DIAMOND PICKAXE

- 29 melee damage
- Finds More Emeralds

Diamond is one of the most durable materials, making it an excellent choice for a pickaxe.

SALVAGE

Finally, the iconic Diamond Pickaxe is available in Minecraft Dungeons as a unique weapon with the built-in effect of finding more emeralds. This sought-after piece of gear can be found as a rare drop in the Redstone Mines level, or the secret Creepy Crypt dungeon.

POWER   SPEED   AREA

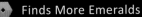

SOUL GATHERING

Your soul meter will appear on the game's main interface below your artifacts—when you have an item equipped that uses them. (This means you won't see your soul meter when first starting the game.)

You earn souls by defeating enemies, and after equipping something which uses souls, you will begin to see these physically float up from defeated enemies and over toward you.

You can then use up souls, lowering the amount in your meter, by activating the particular artifact you have equipped which uses them.

36 ⚄ COMMON
HARVESTER

When used, the Harvester releases souls in an explosion.

- ⚔ 473 artifact damage
- ☀ 4 second cooldown
- ⚀ +1 Soul Gathering
- ⚀ Requires Souls

The Harvester siphons the souls of the dead, before releasing them into a cluster hex of power.

The most common souls-using artifact is the Harvester, which looks like a blue book with a white soul face on it. It provides a powerful detonation over a large area, damaging any enemy nearby.

Our top recommendation for another soul-using artifact is the Corrupted Beacon, which fires a hugely powerful beam of energy in the direction you select. It can quickly sap the life from bosses, and is particularly potent against tougher enemies like the Evoker and Enderman you would normally try to attack from range.

33 ⚄ COMMON
CORRUPTED BEACON

Fires a high-powered beam that continuously damages mobs.

- ⚔ 513 artifact damage per second
- ☀ 2.5 second cooldown
- ⚀ +1 Soul Gathering
- ⚀ Requires Souls

The Corrupted Beacon holds immense power within. It waits for the moment to unleash its wrath.

36 ⚄ COMMON
SOUL HEALER

Heals the most injured ally nearby, including yourself.

- ⚔ 137 health healed
- ☀ 5 second cooldown
- ⚀ +1 Soul Gathering
- ⚀ Requires Souls

Many pieces of gear include soul bonuses, even if they do not use souls themselves. The Feral Soul Crossbow, for example, gives +2 Soul Gathering, increasing the number of souls you will collect. Use several items with such bonuses together and the effects quickly stack up.

As always, it's good to experiment with different combinations of artifacts and armor to find the best build that works for your particular playstyle. There are good souls-based options for both ranged and melee fighters—just remember to always keep an eye on your souls meter. Whenever you are about to enter a boss fight, it's a good idea to have cleared the previous area of smaller enemies to keep your souls stash well stocked.

ACHIEVEMENT AND TROPHY GUIDE

Everyone loves the sight of an Xbox Achievement or PlayStation Trophy appearing on their screen—so here's our guide to getting them all. Tick them off when you're done!

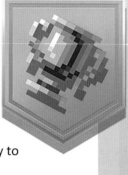

You'll unlock most awards from simply playing through the game, though one or two stand out as particularly tricky. You'll need to beat the game on its top Apocalypse difficulty to unlock its toughest award.

One award in this list requires you to revive a downed friend 20 times—but you can complete this yourself if you have a second controller spare. Our tip is to visit Redstone Mines and revive your second character after getting hit by a minecart!

The full list of Achievements and Trophies lies below:

☐ **LIFE OF THE PARTY**
Revive a downed friend 20 times.

☐ **WOODEN SWORD**
Defeat 50 mobs.

☐ **DIAMOND SWORD**
Defeat 2,500 mobs.

☐ **PASSIVE AGGRESSIVE**
Defeat 50 passive mobs.

☐ **BREAK THE SPELL**
Defeat 50 enchanted mobs.

☐ **SCRAPPY SCOUT**
Reach Level 10.

☐ **APPRENTICE ADVENTURE**
Reach Level 25.

☐ **EXPERT EXPLORER**
Reach Level 50.

☐ **FANCY THAT!**
Find and open your first "fancy" treasure chest.

☐ **MORE FOR ME**
Open 100 treasure chests.

☐ **CHA-CHING!**
Collect a total of 1,000 emeralds.

☐ **OOOH! SHINY!**
Collect a total of 5,000 emeralds.

☐ **OM NOM NOM**
Eat 200 food items.

☐ **HAPPY CAMPER**
Complete Squid Coast and set up camp.

☐ **OUT OF THE WOODS**
Complete Creeper Woods.

☐ **THE PLOT THICKENS**
Complete Pumpkin Pastures and Soggy Swamp.

☐ **BUILT ON SAND, SET IN STONE**
Complete Redstone Mines and Cacti Canyon.

☐ **HIGH AND DRY**
Complete Desert Temple, Fiery Forge, and Highblock Halls.

☐ **SAVED THE OVERWORLD**
Defeat the Arch-Illager at the Obsidian Pinnacle.

☐ **HIGH TREASON**
Defeat the Arch-Illager on Apocalypse.

☐ **BLAST RADIUS**
Kill any 10 mobs at once with TNT.

☐ **MAXED OUT AND GEARED UP**
Equip a gear set consisting of fully enchanted items.

☐ **WORKED LIKE A CHARM**
Enchant an item and upgrade the enchantment to Tier 3.

☐ **A FRIEND IN NEED**
Use artifacts to summon the Wolf, Llama, and Iron Golem at least once each.

EXPAND YOUR ADVENTURE!

Beaten everything Minecraft Dungeons has to offer? Well, just like Minecraft itself, Dungeons is continually evolving.

If you've defeated the Arch-Illager at the end of Minecraft Dungeons' story, you'll know that the tale still isn't quite over. What happens next is explored through a further two expansions, available separately.

Jungle Awakens and Creeping Winter add another set of new levels, new armor, and—most importantly— new pets.

Jungle Awakens takes place on a new island inspired by Minecraft's jungle biome, where you'll find ocelots, parrots and pandas.

New levels include a dingy jungle and an overgrown temple, where you'll find the local fauna may not always be friendly...

Creeping Winter, meanwhile, features an icy fjord and a frozen fortress. Hey, the cold never bothered us anyway!

Icy Creepers and frozen zombies patrol its icy islands, along with the friendlier polar bear and an adorable arctic fox.

If you own Minecraft Dungeons' Hero Edition, you'll have access to these expansions included as part of your game. Otherwise, a pass can be purchased to unlock the two and continue your quest.

79

GOOD LUCK
OUT THERE,
ADVENTURER!